C000162823

ANOTHER
VESSEL OF SELF

SHEA KENYON

Copyright © 2023 Shea Kenyon

All rights reserved. No part of this book may be
reproduced or used in any manner without written
permission of the copyright owner except for the use
of quotations in a book review. For more information,
address: sheakpoetry@gmail.com

First paperback edition December 2023

Published independently by Shea Kenyon

ISBN 979-8-8659-8150-3 (paperback)

For all my loved ones

The flavour of anticipation is one of a completely immersive and unique potency; ingest it, immerse yourself in it, truly feel what is to come

Contents

INTRODUCTION

Another Vessel of Self is as the title suggests: it is an extension of myself, another me. All of my thoughts, desires, feelings, wants, and emotions have bled onto the page for years to create this other sense of being. A living, breathing book of poetry that is as much a part of me as anything else. Each subsection in this book displays my evolution as a person, they personify each peak and trough of my existence. Every lucid sunset that I have gazed upon and each hollow night that has engulfed me is personified in word. It is me, and I am it.

ILLUSIONS CRUMBLE

My first and earliest poems. The barriers begin to crumble. Life is starting to be seen as it truly is. My mind begins to talk amongst itself and internal battles start here that still prevail to this day. These contain the mantra of toppling naivety. The confusion of my human psyche is displayed heavily here. Everything was changing and the world felt new—new and confused.

'A late-night image'

A gentle breeze drifts across your back
As you stare into a full yet empty space in the
distance
Your face remains expressionless
A dark figure emerges
Its presence creates a sense of fear within you
But as the seconds pass
The fear subsides
Its presence becomes fruitful

It asks you to undress
Take the layers off your own body and soul
Strip your ego, your internal voice, your mind full
of chores
All burdens have been erased
A spiritual experience is about to take place.
One enlightening moment

For just a second
You are fulfilled
And have become
In love with existence

'Frenzy'

The moonbeams glare upon your back
You have been chosen to reflect tonight
Chosen to relive moments of the past

The crisp, brittle leaves make a distinct sound
A sound that coincides with one that resides
Within your brain
It resembles a frenzy within you
One that can be calmed with breathing
And the thought of a better time
Or the blissful future
But it cannot be eradicated

You come to the end of your journey
Having passed through every crevice
Of the madman's circus
The weak orange lights
Each thought that you had
Only changed your perception of the street, the
world, the people
Nothing is brightened
Only darkened, perhaps

At any moment
You feel as though you could be lifted

Placed back into the reality above
Far gone from the joke that your friends have
played on you

This eternal twisted thought
Eternal twisted existence

'Momentary lapse'

Flashing in my mind of days gone by
Flashes in my brain, I think I'm going insane
Flashing up ahead, am I being mislead?
Distorted mind, distorted high
Distorted mind, distorted life

The ruthless recollection of a moment
Of innocent wonder
The flash with a wall-like stature
The lock of the labyrinth,
The stoppage of progression,
A holt in mental stability—
A flash of a time past that my mind wishes to
mention
To itself

Flashes of evil
Flashes of greed
Flashes making me internally bleed.
The blood of my soul
The slow deterioration of an unstable body of
words and worry
Enslaved by milk and honey

Loss of life

Paint me on
Wipe it off
Happy until flashes occur
Until they conquer
My mind

Mind hears her
Or him, me
Myself
Argue, mash yourself together till the words are
written
And the man falls down some more
Until there isn't anything to drop down to. Not
even the floor

And he is gone.
As quick as the flash
That lived with him for so long.
You'd think his decision was rather rash
But good for him
For the future of his existence is in the hands of
Himself
And nobody else. Not even the darkest of entities
Only him. Only his true form
That has been gracefully reborn

'The Lost Poet'

The lost poet may never be found;
Their words of beauty, horror, sorrow may forever
stay encapsulated
The fear of no connection may forever haunt them
The shackles of mind may never free them into the
wild

Restless in mind, art within the heart
Death before the words are released
Oh, sweet connection
Forever lost, not once discovered

The words are within a glass cage
They can be seen
But never held,
Never grasped—
Never fully understood.
Questions will always remain
It's never found
The radiant connection never acted upon

Die down
Like the meaning of the words
As they travel through time
And mind.

Warping,
Becoming distorted
And losing their essence;
Misunderstood more and more.
They now wander aimlessly
With an undiscovered attachment

Surrounded by love
Love, so unattainable
A connection so hard to catch at the right moment

Washed up on the shore
Never to be stumbled upon
The link never drawn

Thoughts, feelings, ideas
Lost in translation

'Questions'

Can you feel this too?
Predetermination
Am I even in control?
The end feels near
There's a blurred vision of my life passing
Right in front of me
What can I do?
Death is within us all
And soon enough it will be released

Predetermined
A concept within my eye
Fuzzy, is it breaking through?
Is it trying to break through?!
Is it breaking through?!
Tell me
Has this already happened?
Death at the end of the wick
Is every change I make to stop this
predetermination
Already predetermined?

A confused soul
Aren't we all?
Is anything special?

Or all just insignificant?
Waiting statically
A movie reel yet to be turned on
Rewound
Restarted
Burned in a darkened back alley

Made to grow old
And forget our true selves
The angst so famous to our own lost soul
More and more is forgotten
Less and less seems significant
Time is going to catch up soon

Food for thought
Constant questions
Is that what we're built for?
A whirlpool within my head
Thought, thought, thought
Drain, drain, drain
Eventually empty
Or full?
Another question to add to the list

Will we ever find out?
Ever learn?
Ever reach the threshold?
And move on
Or is the cycle not over yet?

Have you gained completeness?
Have you learned
Over all of these do-overs
What it takes to be perfectly virtuous?
Or is it time
For another rewind?
Another rebirth?
Another run through?
To learn all that shall be learned
To reach that long thought of threshold
And to move on to the world above
Beyond the loop

BEGINNING TO BE CONSUMED

The writing of this period is one of a man who is being eaten by his surroundings. He lays in near constant reflection, gazing toward a horizon in which he wishes would bear some light— light that never seems to arrive. During this time period I was a walking corpse, burdened by a constant weight, an existential dread; my eyes seemed to always tell a story of gloom, of perpetual sadness.

'Here I land, and here I lay'

Here I land, and here I lay
Staring forth to find a way
Lost in thought, I race around
Out of the lock, but nothing's found

Watch and blank to free my mind
Always spinning, running out of time
A hamster wheel, going round and round.
My head a rollercoaster
The lock the fear
Change of heart all through the year

Bedroom woe
Nothing's done
More and more of my thoughts to come
The greatest gift
Can sometimes be a burden
Sit here so long, I hear the birds chirping

Lonely evening,
Bedroom woe
Sulk in sadness,
Succumb to madness
Run off into the bright future
Or sink into the dark oblivion.

Everything lost
I lay on the ground
Face on the brittle moss—
So much loss of self

Dark thought,
Weighing me down
A sandbag pulling me toward the ground
Six feet under
My mind digging its own grave,
Leaving it to be encircled,
By thought and irrational reason,
Progressing further with every season

I have
Sunk
Into the heavy feeling,
Falling further and further on my own
Laying here all alone, thought within me
Leaves its home; or stays to hold.
The thoughts have taken their toll

Plummeting
Toward the end of the dark fog
Until I've been fully engulfed—
All around, the eerie mist.
In search of an exit,
But to no avail
Drifting off,
Quietly

With the thought of an exit, still there
The thought of what could have been, still
prominent
The fear of what might become
Ringing through my brain

Here I am
And here I've stayed
Searching 'round to find a way
I'll leave here some day
Hopefully

'Incomprehensible'

Float off out of mind
Into the sky
See what you cannot see with plain vision
Fruitful or fruitless,
Love or loveless,
Our infinite is endless

Eerie darkness,
With soft, light glimmers of beauty
Vast, wide, colossal infinity
Infinity we cannot understand
Infinity too widely massive
For our maximum comprehension

'A late night bike ride'

A late-night bike ride through the town
Two deformed figures, stuck to the ground, stare
from a distance
They appear to have a thirst for malicious action

The streetlights shine upon you, as if on a podium
Colosseum, Roman games
Shame or fame
Time comes with tragedy
Asleep are many as you grow more conscious
Too conscious for your own liking

Deep below your feet, your wheels,
There's another war
Another action of anger
More death
Dirt stained with blood, intertwined
From the past, the present, and soon, the future

Accelerate
Everything is now moving faster
Distorted sights, distorted sounds
A fuzzy screech you'll find,
A slanted tunnel surrounds your meek mind
The whirls of the wind, filling your ears

The rush taking over, the fire fuelled with an
explosion
As you experience
The power of yourself

The fire inside, the beauty, the life begins to
dampen
Darkness has taken over
At ease no more

Distorted chatter,
Incoherent, wavy, mindful breaking chatter
The words are moving faster, in all directions,
Through all different forms, volumes
Self-torment—
Brain numbing torment
Louder, Louder,
It becomes more and more incoherent
Until it is cracked back to reality

The worms squirm with their intent
As do you at the thought of their discomfort
Upon reflection of this journey,
You consider thoughts that weren't present
They open you even further
We have entered the operation room
Dismantle, dissect past experiences
Your mind has been opened for reflection
Overthinking has now begun

Accelerate
The thoughts, the worry, the fear of itself,
accelerate
A crash course within the mind
Obstacles to face,
Shackles to break,
Free yourself from this fettered existence

Plaguing your thoughts
Leave you distraught
You're going, you're going
And you're off...
The spring wasn't enough
And now you're falling,
Into the void
Spiralling into the abyss

A late-night bike ride through the town
Two deformed figures, stuck to the ground, stare
from a distance
Imaginary is what they are
A fallacy
An image created on the grounds of delusion
Deceitful self,
A twisted head; twist off the sanity
It's crazy to think how warped a mind can become
How differently a man can perceive an object, a
scene,
While his mind is twisting
How much he can think about agony

The madness can truly accelerate when it wants to;
The mind can twist further and further
Until it must be sedated by its own self
If not, it is left to spiral deeper into the pit, without
any help
Beginning to melt,
Beginning to melt
Ending all sense of self...
Gone and eventually forgotten

'Compulsion'

I taste blood as I swallow,
Though I have not bled;
Ulcer of mind
Instructs you how to feel

Swallow again
Now I taste no blood
I know that it's phony;
Yet I do as you tell me

I do as you tell me,
Though nothing good comes;
Only more of your control,
More of your fun

Pain within me
No sacrifice made
Only more for you to numb;
My pleasures to come

'The valley of hope'

Soft trees;
The grass all green
Free,
Free
Is all I want to be
Free of burden
Free of time
Free of words that seem to rhyme

I want to let go of that hollow yet heavy feeling
And feel the liberation
Of a soul unfettered

The whirling wind
The shadow cast
At such ease that does not last
All I hope for is that the clouds will pass

In the valley of hope
Shines a thoughtful sun
It lets us know
The war of the internal
Is all but won
The sun—it shines with a great optimism;
It glows with a certain beauty

And the once exuberant, energised soul
Begins to radiate once more

There is so much wonder,
So much love,
So much hope
That comes to life
When the door to a better state
Does not remain closed

'Oh, Memories'

Oh, Memories
Such a sweet yet sly construct
To cherish a memory, to look back fondly
To see a gracious time through two sets of eyes.
It can be so delightful to reminisce
But it can be a backward love,
A twisted longing
Hurt and pain within the wonderful,
The moment
There to never be held again
Falling through your hands
Like the sand of dreams
A grain, a memory made, a time no more
Each grain a moment—gone with the wind

This fondness for old
Memories of past
Can feel almost bitter
When compared to the present
The beauty of then contrasting with the dreary
now
This outreach shadowed by the realisation
That it has gone forever
And the now is the only

Oh, Memories
Turned to dust
Left to float off with the world
To land,
To regrow into more pure wonder
To faintly retrace the stages of gain and loss,
Love and trust
And to come to an end,
As all things must

Oh, Memories
I was wrong.
I must cherish you
Until we go;
Before our regrowth.
No matter what

'Around the fire'

Around the fire we dance.
Morbidly
Without care
A crash course—
One that ends in us being engulfed in hatred, in
pain
There is no one else to blame

Around the fire we dance
Lament for us
We are in a trance
Around we go,
Again, and again—
Hold each other.
Languidly we walk
Full of loathing and sorrow
You may see no substance on the surface
But behind the eyes there is woe;
All of us
Lost in a trance
Stuck in the dance

There is pain behind those eyes
Reveal your worries, wishes, loves of life
With who you walk this plane with

Nothing phoney,
Nothing fake
We're stuck in the same place
Without a meaning, without a trace—
Not sure what we'll come to face.
Unveil yourself to one another
Take in others as your sister or your brother,
Or a mate,
A lover

Around the beauty we lust;
Within the beauty we love
Walk amongst others
Parade over the pile of sinister sights
And stroll within the true bliss
Surrounded with what's right,
Within what shall be admired.
Fuck the hatred
Fuck the lust without the love
Fuck everything where the immoral prevails

We should celebrate our freedom,
Parade over the restrictions
Love another
Appreciate all the divine beauty of one's self
See this divine beauty in all
And cherish it

We may be aimless souls around the fire

With fear and anxiety of what may become the
present
Or we may be wandering with purpose in being,
With mindful certainty

But what is shared is this confusing existence
Where we all dance and shift around
A fire of golden opportunity.
Full of selfless freedom
That shall be adored

Love our aims
Or lack thereof—
Who cares if something is aimless?
Help it find meaning, clarity
That is what we all must do
All of us gathered here today,
Tomorrow,
And the next day
But hopefully not for all eternity

VERGING ON

The themes of this subsection are desolate. Verging On is compiled with reference to themes of isolation, madness, and loneliness; much of it philosophical in nature. Verging On is chosen as a title for this subsection as it explains the time period and my psyche within that period perfectly. Verging on love, but it is never attained. Verging on a full life, but it remains dull. On the edge of the ledge, the difference is in front of you, but the leap is never taken. Not to love, not to life, not to death—everything remains the same, desolate, but nothing is ever quite over. There must be hope!

'Summer rain'

I was warm
In that moment, I felt calm
Pleasant, easy going
But you had to appear.
I must say hello—
I must play your twisted game,
As I do not wish to end up with a twisted fate.
I wish for you to not feast on my being.
All the gloom that I have left
Is withering into complete darkness

Why must you arrive?
To rot the little amount of soulful life left within
me
To erase my grain of hope.
I am so far from even content.
All that my mind has left
Is fading into horrible despair

Do not take that from me
I do not wish to arrive back in the same old spot
Sullen and empty
No substance left;
Nothing to fight the good fight
Nothing but a flourishing thought

Which arrives once in a blue moon,
Inevitably stripped from a gripping hand
Which gets weaker by the day;
The blooming thought already awaits its demise.
A fire not fuelled
Left to burn into nothingness

My nothingness,
So far from even content.
As I hastily walk the valleys of relative misery
The true demise awaits
Around a long, painfully drawn out corner
A slow burn out,
So inelegant—
A snail, crossing the path
The slow train, slipping towards the end of the
track
Anticipating the soft crunch
The ending of such existence.

The train
Into the ravine
The mind
Falling out of love—
Love for life
And what is left after that?

'Sick with solitude'

I recall when I was filed down some more
Sheds of my being
Falling right before my eyes
Like the skin of a reptile
Floating down to lay in front of me
My head bowed in misery
My eyes staring at the lost essence
The moment burned in time
For a short while.
Not dissimilar
To anything prior.
Sick with solitude
Nowhere to go

The desire for another beautiful moment
Is fading in the restless night
More of my time,
My energy
My substance
Is fading in the restless night
The beauty, ready to disappear
The meaning, about to shift
To another plane of thought,
The one with no exit;
With no escape.

Where can I even go?
What can I even do?
Sick with solitude
There's nowhere to go

I am missing all the beauty that is to be seen
Day by day, losing the essence of what it is to just
be.
I look left, right, up toward the Heavens;
But I see no way out
So, my head sinks into my hands once more
To again be filled with doubt.
I want to leave
There are so many places to be
So many faces to see—
Though all that I am faced with is the ground
beneath me

And all I feel is my head bulging with all that is
pent up within my soul:
The sadness, the anger, the frustration
I wish it'd flee and free its home.
I sit here and look around
Left, right, up at the Heavens
Asking myself once again,
What can I even do?
I'm sick with solitude
And there is nowhere to go

'To the fullest'

Life, a rollercoaster
As they say
Rise and fall,
Ascend to descend
You reach a peak;
You slowly, smoothly flow back from the heights,
As you believe happiness will appear once more.

But in this moment
I am falling once again;
With no up in sight
Dragged compliantly with the minutes that fly
past.
Time, a structure
Flying by like the image
On the outside of a train
Contorted,
Feeling as though you can't really see it,
Can't really feel it
Can't really feel.
It comes and goes
Barely observed,
Hardly experienced

Senselessly sitting as you move forward

Almost frozen in place,
Feeling as though
There is no real reason to move—
The lack of feeling becoming less than a rare
occurrence
Indifferent to all that surrounds you.
Everything outside of you
In near vision
Within the concept of time itself
Moves on without a care, or a thought
As they do not feel as you feel;
A head has bowed, eyes toward the table below
The abyss presents its mindless poverty to you

It has almost become a ritual performed.
Staring toward the emptiness below,
The emptiness ahead,
The emptiness all around.
Fate?
I don't want to accept this
A life half lived
A time,
A space,
A love
Thrown toward a wall of nothingness
A wall which was bestowed upon me
By all that has been endured.
Please don't let me accept this as my fate;
A life half lived
Substance drained out—

Only a shadow of life left
With no sun of rebirth present
No sun of life
To shine
Its magnificent light
To lift me up
Oh, so gradually

I don't want to feel this slow, numbing decline.
Love for life fading,
Deteriorating,
Into a puddle of what makes us whole—
I am no longer complete.

What I wish—is to rise once more,
And again, feel the love of a life
So majestically full
To be at peace with the life that surrounds me,
Living life as if it were always filled with bliss
Embracing all thrown this way.
I wish to always be
Smiling in a heavenly moment,
Knowing it will be a warm memory
Cherished tomorrow, and each day after

I hope to rise again
Emerging from a pit of despair
Shooting off—
Away from the hopelessness,
Away from the numbing feeling of nothingness.
I hope to rise again

To feel the love from a life worth living
A life lived to the fullest

'A sea of pain'

A sea of pain
From which I arrived
A sea of pain
In which I stare so blankly at
My face has become submerged
I am now beneath—
At least from what I see.
But I feel no death;
I feel nothing.
Are they the same?

A river of blood flows in the same old fashion.
No change of course, no rush, no thrill
So stagnant
No movement;
No chance
A gamble
That cannot be had.
No mystery
No love, no lust.
I know where it'll head—
Another lost kingdom

Am I the same?
My body, engulfed

Instant death;
Instant nothing
Handed down to you

This is already what
Is.
And is it all that will be?
Everything that flows—
A sea of nothing
With no thrill, no love, no life
Drifting sorrowfully
So Empty,
So Empty,
So Empty

'A Morning Sight'

An empty carousel spins
On the other side of my window
Murky light,
Foggy mist
Our day will soon come

'The prolonged wait'

The prolonged wait may never end
Your blissful life may never start
Eerie darkness may forever stay
Until you reach
Your inevitable grave

A New Movement

Aspark has flown and created with it a drive for change, for understanding. The new movement is focused on defeating those accountable for sorrow and dissolution. This drive for change is fuelled by a hatred for monotony. A burning passion for experience resonates through each poem. Alcohol and insanity are catalysts for original thought; they're reflected in the work of this time.

'Wisdom'

What is life
But a mesmerising self-reflection?
Countless thoughts—
A consumption of experience
And of dread.
A timeline of questions
A pursuit of reason.
Discovery;
Which is virtuous, which is not?
Do the answers matter?
Relentless.

Should I be so unthoughtful toward existence?
Is the key to withholding such contradictions—
Such persistent pursuit for meaning—
Just to shy away?
To comfort the self?
To keep the mind at a level of servitude
Imposed on oneself
To never question reality,
To never think
With such undeniable passion?

Do I dare not cross the paths and journey the trail
of why?

Shall I feed myself with constant comfort
And wallow in the less than content
To never let that current pull me away?

Shall I live with it all?
And relish in passion
For all the questions that find themselves forming
in existence?
Embrace, embrace
Such thought
Oh, such experience.
I will become wiser by the minute
For the glowing leaves of wisdom
Flow on through with each and every occurrence.
Their impact may not show from the first
unknowing absorption
Or the conscious realisations of mind,
But together they will build to make one's
philosophy;
Their
Reasons for living
Their
Loves, desires, truths
And all the reflections within…

With all, I will journey on through
Toward the full life,
With hunger for living,
Relentless ardour for the path,
Knowingly pondering along the way.

For if I cannot ponder,
I cannot live.
If I cannot question,
How do I know I am?
If I cannot feel,
I would become numb to reality.
And ask
Am I really alive?

But if I look,
Pursue,
Take in the lessons from all experiences
Listen to the words of sages
Then pen my own.
I would hope my wisdom would grow
With sweet intensity—

For it is the pursuit of wisdom
Not the search for meaning.
The road to knowledge—to deep reflection
Not the need for a reason, to exist.
The former of each; the path to take
And they will be, forever,
My cause

'The music isn't over, it's only just begun'

The memory fades
With every flying moment
Slowly
Like a poem in the early hours of a non-existent
afternoon
After its creation in the mind—
Thought-racing mind of an early morning
Wrought with pictures, images, verses of
experience
Meant to be written;
Wished to be had.
They fade in the endless morning
The endless dark, reflective evening.

In the night,
Opportunity gone—
It'll be there in the future
Perhaps.
I wish not to wait
I wish not to wait
I'm not going to wait;
We want the world
And we want it
Now

'Everything else is in-between'

I have a few hours left
Before the death of the day
Comes to claim such wondrous optimism

I have a few hours left
Before the end of an in-between night,
Where fortuity and want have not had an
opportunity
To be let loose
To be freed.
Not a chance,
To play their own slick set of cards

I have a few hours left
Before the end of an in-between night
In which there has been not a drop,
Not even a fragment of possibility
To taste the sweet unknown—
Ah, the sweet taste of all the living—
All the living, not yet known to me

I have a few hours left
Until the stoppage of the mystery, the unknown
Comes to take all hope back

'Revel'

I wonder if there are still people roaming the
streets
It's someone's death night.
Sullen men,
Sullen guys
Wandering in search of meaning
Gone—
No obituary

Unknown lives
Adorations of past
Flow on through the air
Oh! How they have gone!
Lost so long ago

The spark in the air
No longer exists to that degree
At least not for now.
Where is the reignition?
It must be brought back
From its dark, unwanted age
Into this ignition
With ever-glowing, over-joyous flavours of life—
Sundance…

Purposelessness births our purpose
A glimmer of clarity shines through.
A flicker of light in the immensity of dark
Wished to be turned into a gorgeous,
Eye widening,
Soul thrilling,
Monstrosity.
The thrill drives the soul

And for all those that wish to feel
The ardour!
They can revel in it all
They can revel in the pursuit
Of the thrill—
The thrill, grasped, from the creation of feeling—
Ah! So alive!
Attaining the immense energy,
Fuelled by want for life;
We can revel in it all

'Unquantified'

I wish to reject the comfort trail
You will not make a nothing of a man!
I wish to revel in unquantified living
And taste unquantified ecstasy
You will not take that away from me!
You will not take the profound path away!

Where is my courage to reject such a trail?
Feed me my courage!
I wish to grasp such courage and to absorb it, to
digest it;
To greater my own self
And to become my own

I want to strive for an abundance of feeling
I want to ingest unquantified feeling
As to not feel the wretchedness of regular
existence—
Which, in reality, is the lack of any true
Thought, feeling or movement,
Though it is rarely perceived as such.
But a man with a lack of true feeling is one so lost
That no passion can save him from such horrible
stability;
It all becomes so futile

I wish to indulge and to feast on all I can grasp
As to reach my own promises of golden words
Of new, wise, insightful outlooks and perceptions
Truths of experience
Discovered on this movement
To conquer and subdue the life of nothing
A tyrannical life that does not make me learned
But creates a man of lesser freedom—
A lesser degree of self

I wish to have the courage to eradicate this trail of
destructive comfort
And to take the journey into a life of unquantified
living;
To feast on it all
And indulge in unquantified ecstasy;
To adore it
To absorb it
To then share the profound, golden words
Discovered from an enquiry into my nature of
being—
Full of ardour,
Pursued with irrepressible passion

'We live and flow and fade away'

We live and flow, and fade away
Eventually.
Prominent, alive, mercilessly flowing and reaching
and grasping;
Wanting,
And then we have expelled all we can within the
joys of society
And solitude takes its place.
Some wants still there
Regrets infiltrate the mind
And fill its void
With hurt and wishes
That were never there,
Never had been, never seemed to be opportune—
It seems they never will

We all fade in the end
Like smoke dissipating in the air
Our everything
Becomes no one's anything.
But we have lived
For that short period.
Which came
And went
Like the pleasures of an evening,

Flying high.
A life was lived
A life was lost
Thoughts were had, spoken
Plans made—
Did they ever come to fruition?
Did you fall in love with your existence?

Words were, however, gained
To be so prominent, or
To fly under the radar?
Regardless,
They were still written into the foundations of
every existence
To be seen and pondered over in the future;
In the loop
Which we all share—
Where we all live and breathe within its
boundaries
At one point or another

After we have expelled all of this immense energy
for life
Into society
And its pleasures have run rife in our minds
And consumed us so fully,
We can reflect
On how we mutually felt something so real—
In soaking up all the wants,
And letting go of all the fetters.

But after all is released, crazed out of our free
minds
Life shall begin to tighten its shackles once more.
What's life when all our wants and desires have
past
Had or not?
Consumed by regret or want for a better time
Reflection,
Or harmful lamentation?
We live and flow, and fade away
Eventually

I HAVE BLED EVERY LAST DROP

Much like that of previous chapters, this subsection is one of reflection. Its difference lies, however, in the sheer amount of life force that has oozed through my veins and onto the page for so many years. Each evolution of my craft mashes together to create this section. My mind bathed in its familiar tortures and ripe conclusions were discovered in turn.

'The eternal summer'

I paid for my money
With my soul and my youth
And let the wasted time eat away at my essence
As I reaped no benefit from giving away the most
finite thing of all,
Grasping for more toward the end;
It can be wasted so easily.
Reaching,
For a drop more,
Just a drop
As the marrow of life dissipates
And the end creeps up oh-so suddenly.
How wretched!
In an eatery of distraction,
Philosophical suicide.
A monotonous monster is bred…

Can I not drink from glacier fountains?
With the soft wind against my skin,
The delicate touch of beauty,
And the adoring rays of sunshine—
Building a fiery passion for life.
My reignited essence,
Zealous in my being.
An open road is laid out before my very eyes

Horizons never looked so wondrous!

Her sun-beamed dress
Always by my side.
I am now at peace with the world,
At one with life
Gazing toward the fascinating horizon
Immersing myself in the totality of the joyous
present
All to enamour

We dance around
In a Garden of Eden
A dance with every sweet soulful delight
Hand in glove
Living as one should live—
In the eternal summer

'Release'

Gather yourselves—
Go toward the garden.
The world awaits you
In hopeful uncertainty

Is it the forbidden fruit
That we must eat?
Or shall we create our own frenzy
With needed insanity
And words fuller than a crying river?
We must leak to release
Every now and then;
To create our art
Which seizes to exist in a world
That we can perceive with meaning.
We create to survive

'Feel'

I worry about the future
All those golden promises
I wish to fulfil

'Dreamland'

Do you not conjure up dreamland?
I'm so lost.
Imagination;
It only takes a few steps to arrive
Although the biggest leaps are soulful, mental
feelings

I look at the damp, dreary streets,
They appear grainy
I cannot fully focus on them.
They're trying to trick you!

I have drifted off unimaginably
I appear dour-faced
Far beneath a land of lyrical vision,
In the lost streets of futures,
Torn away!

'Poison'

I'm going to jump and flail and scream
For the tormenting piglets
Sneer, huck and laugh
In the light that is my mind.
They spit and snotter their verbal inward torture
A mental drowning to which you must flounder
slowly
To fully regain stature
And enter a peaceful solitude
Away from their clutches;
This process may become eternal—
Perpetually draining

Their guise of piglets hath appeared to me
As they try to batter through defences,
Attempt to poison idyllic waters
And future familiar landscapes
With a cutthroat mentality

Even now as I write
They wish for me to erase
Each resonating word,
Every fervorous explanation,
Each allegory and metaphor
That runs as true as the rivers
Flowing so sweetly

In the lost forests of alpine love,
Far secluded from corruption.
Deeply entrenched in
Solace, ecstasy…

Snapping back at myself
At war with images,
A clash of consciousness,
I jolt inwardly
To defeat those accountable
And regain mental posture.

Do the words I wrote affect?
Me, all, everything?
Are they paramount to my judgement?
Will they devour and consume?
They will try and lead you to believe!
Gnawing away at the brain in a guerrilla battle
Where you're treated with contempt.
They cloud a clear, blue sky
With harmful deceit

Will they scorn me for this?
Puppeteer my surroundings egregiously?
The paranoia might just ingest me!
Envelop my whole being.
No! Never, Never!
I'll regain the power, the control,

Strike them down on their pillage of my soothing tranquillity
And I'll lead them all to the slaughterhouse!

'Summer's night'

Summer's night
Our innocence is now lost
The harsh truth of reality
Has fallen upon us
Like a ruthless, crashing wave
Lost in the uncontrolled motion.
Can't find any bearings anymore

We're all gone from the fields
Where it all used to live and be.
The vast
Here's there's and everywhere's
No simple evening light
To transcend
Bathed in the fresh summer air—
Calm as can be.
Peace was found in your chaos

Summer's night,
Where did you go?
I must sit in your absence
As grapes grow for wine
Never drunk
Sun beams for skin
Never touched

Smiles breed for eyes
Paned by love's absence

Summer's night,
Where did you go?
We've been expelled from your boundaries
And another avenue is never to be found

'The New Gods'

The new gods are devices—
Devices of control
Fallen angels—devils
We're being told what to see and what to believe
We are pawns in their relentless grinder.
Our minds are a decaying battlefield;
Ground is lost every day.

When self-confrontation occurs
When a moment of stillness falls over a sky,
Obsessed by whirling winds
Trenches are dug
And we bury ourselves in the numb.
True light lays before our eyes
If only we could really see.

The eatery of distraction
Sends our souls to temporary graves of vanity
Our perception, our mindful presence
Burns painfully to empty.
So many moments have been hollowed by the
poisonous fruits on offer.

The universe lost the power of chance
The human lost the power to ponder;

We lost the second in the park,
Where the eyes caught one another, delicately, as
we fell
From the tender, sensitive cliffs of understanding
Toward the dread.
We consistently give up minutes and minutes of
Touch, laugh, talk, dance
Without a second thought.
When glanced at with outside eyes
We must see that we subdue our existence to
nothing but motion;
Blank, desireless self-tyranny

Every inch of territory stolen,
Each millisecond of time squandered to such futile
endeavours is
A tragedy
But a tragedy to which we amplify
By choosing to deprive ourselves
From the sacred flavours of our life
With every chance we get
In worship of the new gods
The fallen angels—devils
That sit so close—within arm's reach
A toxin to the magic of the senses,
A cancer of the present

'We set the scene'

Once summer has flung us its mesmerising waves
A drink in autumn
Is needed to cool the tide.
The calm, almost melodic air;
It has this energy, this feature—
It transports you back
To a time of simple pleasures;
A sunken warmth irradiates your being.
These simple pleasures are, for now,
Life's only consumer

The grass, it lays slightly thick
It hasn't been cut for a short while
An air of nostalgia fills the lungs
And eases its way into the bloodstream;
Creating, with it, a gelatine heart.

Impulse is rife
Its intensity heightens
Then begins to fly on through.
The moon slowly ascends
The sun leaves its soft traces in the sky
Delicate creatures gather
An aura of chance sets the scene

'Idle Misfortune'

I am the spectator
Of my own failure
I stand aware, and yet I stand dormant
As I sense the shards of glass
Penetrate my skin
And drain me for all I am worth;
A tiny speck of blood

'The Bridge to Change has Collapsed'

Quickly in the room
You hear the pitch shift
From noisy fractional decadence
To sombre dissolution—
Dissolving,
Your Forever now resides
Within the miserably dull

A hollowed being emerges
From the dust clouds of fallacy.
It is you
Shrivelled and sullen
A shadow from the blackest of alleys;
Prowess no longer rules this world.
Its yet another human sacrifice!
Maybe in another life, my friend

'Pardon'

I pardon myself every day
On the grounds of youthful folly
But as the sun rises,
After each dusk has fallen and settled
The once exuberant soul smokes out,
And chokes on its own diminishment;
Falling to its knees
Its throat is now to be slit in ceremonial fashion

Youth dwindles, dies
Veracity gulps down its last drop.
Indulgence falls to the sword of mute carefulness.
Delight is only viewed on horizons looking
backward.
Our youth is an immeasurable masterpiece
But once it has been truly vanquished,
Blessed my skin with its final dusk,
Stagnant horrors will christen the days that come
to pass.
The world becomes a delicate cocoon
No longer a place to be conquered
With velocity and prowess;
We deteriorate with these attributes

Obediently we embed ourselves into motionless
evil
We are no longer our movement; Idleness is our
reality
We're nothing but a constructed falsehood
Fading in the restless night

Printed in Great Britain
by Amazon

35958903R00046